OXFORD BOOKWO **PRICE: $20.00 (3798/abbarp)**
Teen Fiction: Romance

Maria's Summer in London

ROWENA WAKEFIELD

Stage 1 (400 headwords)

Illustrated by Laura Perez

Series Editor: Rachel Bladon
Founder Editors: Jennifer Bassett
and Tricia Hedge

OXFORD
UNIVERSITY PRESS

Great Clarendon Street, Oxford, OX2 6DP, United Kingdom

Oxford University Press is a department of the University of Oxford.
It furthers the University's objective of excellence in research, scholarship,
and education by publishing worldwide. Oxford is a registered trade
mark of Oxford University Press in the UK and in certain other countries

This simplified edition © Oxford University Press 2018

The moral rights of the author have been asserted

First published in Oxford Bookworms 2018

10 9 8 7 6 5 4 3 2 1

ISBN: 978 0 19 402277 4

A complete recording of this Bookworms edition of
Maria's Summer in London is available.

Printed in China

Word count (main text): 5,845

For more information on the Oxford Bookworms Library,
visit www.oup.com/elt/gradedreaders

ACKNOWLEDGEMENTS

Cover images: Getty Images (teen girl/Mikolette); Shutterstock (London doodles/Saint A),
(London illustration/balabolka)

The publisher would like to thank the following for their permission to reproduce photographs:
123RF pp.46 (London bus/Fedor Selivanov), 46 (Westminster/Paul Hampton), 47 (Tower Bridge/
Tomas Marek), 47 (London Eye/Michal Bednarek); Alamy Stock Photo p.58 (restaurants and shops/
travellinglight); Getty Images pp.46 (Tower of London/Bjorn Holland), 46 (Nelson's Column/
Eurasia/robertharding), 58 (students/Cultura RM Exclusive/Nancy Honey), 58 (Brighton Pier/
Laurence Cartwright Photography); Oxford University Press p.47 (Buckingham Palace/r.nagy)

Illustrations by: Laura Perez, Anna Goodson Illustration Agency

CONTENTS

MAP OF LONDON

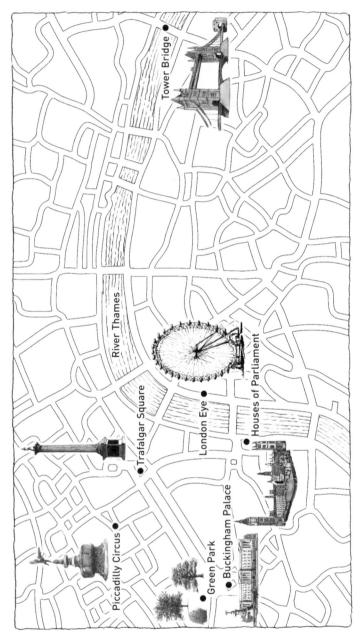

Tower Bridge

River Thames

London Eye

Houses of Parliament

Trafalgar Square

Piccadilly Circus

Green Park

Buckingham Palace

Chapter 1
Hello England

It's seven o'clock in the evening, and Maria is at Pamplona Airport. Her plane leaves in thirty minutes, and she feels sick. She's going to a summer school in London, and she's going to learn English there. She's fifteen, and this is her first time in England and her first time away from her family. Away from her mum and dad, her friends, her dog, and her brother for three weeks. Three weeks! And for all that time, she can't speak any Spanish – only English.

She's going to stay at the home of an English woman called Claire. A Polish girl is staying there too, and Claire is going to meet Maria and the Polish girl at the airport. Maria has lots of questions in her head. Is Claire going to be nice? Is the Polish girl going to be nice? And the food! Is she going to like the food? Her friend Isabella went to London last summer and she ate potatoes every day. And sausages and eggs for breakfast!

But now she needs to get on the plane. Maria feels very alone. She said goodbye to her mum and dad half an hour ago, and she can't stop thinking about them. On the plane, she's sitting next to a man and a woman, and they're speaking in English. Maria listens to them. They're speaking very fast and Maria can't understand them. Is she going to understand any of the people in

England? She looks out of the window at the blue skies of Pamplona. *Adiós España*, she thinks. Goodbye Spain.

* * *

When Maria arrives in London, it's raining. At the airport, Claire is waiting for her. She's about forty, with dark hair and a big smile. The Polish girl is with her. She's older than Maria perhaps, about sixteen. She has long brown hair, and beautiful big green eyes. She looks very excited, not nervous like Maria.

'Hello, Maria!' says the woman. 'I'm Claire, and this is Emilia.'

'Hello,' says Emilia, and she smiles at Maria.

'How was your flight, Maria?' asks Claire.

Maria doesn't understand.

'The plane?' says Claire. 'Was it OK?'

'*Sí*. Sorry, yes,' Maria says. 'Thank you.'

'Good. OK, let's go and find my car,' says Claire.

They get into the car, and Claire asks the girls a lot of questions. Is this their first time in England? Where do they want to go in London? What food do they like? Emilia answers Claire's questions, but Maria is quiet. She feels afraid. She doesn't want to speak English, because she doesn't want to say the wrong thing. She looks out of the window through the rain. It's beginning to get dark. Everything here is different: the roads, the buildings, the shops, the trees! There are lots of houses, not flats like in Spain, and they look very old.

'Hello, Maria! I'm Claire, and this is Emilia.'

After about an hour, they arrive at Claire's home – a house in Clapham, in south London. All the houses in the street are white, with big front windows. Claire's house has a red front door, and there are lots of flowers in the front garden.

When they go into the house, Claire and Emilia take off their shoes. That's strange, thinks Maria, but she takes off her shoes, too. It's very different to Maria's home. There's carpet in every room. There is a room

After about an hour, they arrive at Claire's home.

for eating called a dining room. And Claire has two gardens! There is one at the front of the house, and one at the back. Claire takes the girls to their rooms. Maria's room isn't big, but it's nice. From the window, she can see the back garden. Her room is next to Emilia's room.

'Tomorrow morning, I'm going to take you to school,' says Claire slowly. 'We need to leave the house at eight fifteen because school begins at nine o'clock.'

'OK. Thank you,' says Emilia.

'Thank you,' says Maria.

'It's late now, so let's eat something and then get some sleep,' says Claire. She makes the girls a sandwich, and then they all say goodnight and go into their rooms.

Maria closes the door. Now she's alone. She listens to the rain, and the noises of London. She gets her phone from her bag and calls home. Her mum answers and Maria begins to cry. She wants to be at home, not here in this strange house and in this strange room. England feels different, it looks different, it smells different. Maria's mum listens to her. Tomorrow is a new day, her mum tells her, and after a good night's sleep, she's going to feel better and have a good time.

'*Te amo*,' she says. I love you.

Maria says goodbye to her mum, and looks out of the window. Three weeks of rain and potatoes. Hello England.

Chapter 2
Summer School

Maria can't sleep that night. She's thinking about school in the morning. Is she going to like it? Is she going to understand the teacher? Then, she hears something. Somebody is crying. Maria gets out of bed and goes to the door. The noise is coming from Emilia's room. Maria is surprised. Emilia looked very happy and excited earlier. Is she really crying now?

Maria goes to Emilia's door. She wants to go in and ask, 'Are you OK?', but she's nervous. Then the noise suddenly stops and the door opens.

'Maria?' says Emilia. She looks angry. 'What are you doing?'

'Sorry,' says Maria. 'I hear… I heard… Are you OK?'

Emilia looks at Maria's face and she smiles. 'Yes. Thank you,' she says. 'My boyfriend: he's in Poland and three weeks is very, very…'

'Long?' asks Maria.

'Yes, very long, and I'm sad.'

Maria wants to say something nice, but she can't think of the words, so she puts her hand on Emilia's arm and smiles. Emilia smiles back.

'Tomorrow, can I sit with you, at school?' asks Emilia.

'Yes, please,' says Maria. They smile and say goodnight. Then Maria goes to her room, and at last, she sleeps.

Maria puts her hand on Emilia's arm and smiles.

In the morning, Maria has breakfast with Claire and Emilia. Before breakfast, she's nervous. She doesn't want to eat sausages and eggs. But Maria is surprised. There's no sausages and eggs on the table. There's bread and coffee, like at home in Spain. Emilia looks happy this morning. She smiles and talks a lot, but Maria is very quiet.

'Did you sleep well, Maria?' Claire asks. 'Do you feel homesick?'

'Homesick?' Maria asks. 'I don't understand, sorry.'

'It's when you are away from home and you miss your family and friends, so you feel sad,' Claire says.

'Perhaps, yes,' says Maria.

'It's OK,' says Claire. 'You're going to have a great time here.'

They are taking the Tube to school. Pamplona does not have underground trains, only buses, so this is something very new for Maria. They walk to the station and then go underground on a long escalator. The escalator goes very far down, and Maria stands behind Claire. It's strange underground and Maria doesn't like it. It's very hot when they are standing and waiting for the train. But Maria suddenly hears a big noise, and then the train arrives.

When everybody gets on the train, there are a lot of people, so Maria, Emilia, and Claire can't sit down. Maria stands near Claire and watches the people. Some are wearing suits, some are wearing T-shirts; some are young, some are old. People are using their phones, reading, or talking with friends. And some are sleeping!

They get off the Tube at a place called Piccadilly Circus. When they come out of the station, there are beautiful old buildings, lots of people, lots of cars – and some big red London buses! The city feels alive and exciting, and Maria begins to feel excited, too. At home in Spain, Maria saw pictures of London in books and on TV shows, and now she's here! It's amazing!

The girls walk down the street with Claire, and look at the shops and the old buildings.

'The school is near a park called Green Park,' says Claire. 'When you walk across the park, you can see Buckingham Palace. We can go there one day.' She stops. 'And here is the school.'

The city feels alive and exciting.

Emilia and Maria go with Claire into a big building.

'Have a good day,' Claire says, 'and meet me here after your last class.'

The girls say goodbye to her, and a woman takes them to their classroom. A teacher is standing at the front of the room.

'Come in! Come in!' he says. 'I'm James, and I'm your teacher.'

Emilia and Maria go and sit together at the back of the classroom. Some more students arrive, and then the class begins.

'OK, I want you to work with the person next to you,' says James. 'You're going to ask them some questions.'

He gives them the questions, and they begin. Emilia looks at Maria. 'Do you want to ask?' she says.

'OK,' says Maria. 'What is your name? I know that. And I know this, too: Where are you from? Poland.'

'Yes,' says Emilia. 'I'm from Warsaw in Poland. It's a big city.'

'OK. How old are you?' asks Maria.

'Sixteen.'

'What do you like doing?'

'Well, I like food and cook. No, cooking,' says Emilia. 'I like cooking.'

'I like cooking, too!' says Maria.

'Oh, you *and* me!' smiles Emilia.

'And I like cooking... what's the word?' says Emilia.

'On television, you watch…'

'Shows?'

'Yes, shows. I like cooking shows.'

'Me too!' says Maria.

They smile. Maria learns a lot about Emilia. She and Emilia both have a younger brother, they both have a dog, they both like music, and they both want to go on a red London bus.

At one o'clock, they go and eat. Emilia gets fish and chips. 'English food!' she laughs. So Maria gets fish and chips too.

'I like cooking, too!'

'It looks good!' says Emilia. 'What do you eat in Spain?'

Maria tells Emilia about the food in Spain. 'My favourite is *tortilla de bacalao*,' she says. 'We make it with eggs and fish – but it's not like this fish! And you? Polish food?'

'My favourite Polish food is *borscht*, but I can't tell you about it in English,' says Emilia. 'I don't know the words!'

'And can you make it?'

'Yes, but not like my mum. My mum makes it very good – no, very well.'

Two Italian students come and sit with Maria and Emilia then, and they ask questions and talk. The students in the class are all between fourteen and seventeen, and they are from many different countries: Brazil, Japan, Saudi Arabia, Colombia, Turkey, and Italy.

Maria listens to Emilia and the Italian students, but she doesn't say a lot.

'Did you like the fish and chips?' asks Emilia.

Maria looks: she ate all of the fish and chips. 'Yes,' she says. 'It was really good!'

* * *

In the afternoon, the students go to Green Park and play football. It's hot, and after the football, Maria and Emilia sit in the sun.

'Your boyfriend – what's his name?' Maria asks.

'Aurek. He's very nice, very... oh, what do you say? Like beautiful, but for boys!'

'Handsome?' says Maria.

Emilia laughs. 'Yes, handsome! Look! I have a photo on my phone.'

Maria looks at the photo. 'He's nice,' she says.

'Do you have a boyfriend?' asks Emilia.

'No.'

'You can find an English boy!' says Emilia.

'No, my English is bad,' says Maria, and Emilia laughs.

'Look! I have a photo on my phone.'

'No! Your English is good.'

'But I'm afraid when I speak English,' says Maria. 'You aren't.'

'Don't be... what did you say? Afraid?' says Emilia.

'Yes.'

'Don't be afraid, Maria!'

At five o clock, school finishes. Maria and Emilia wait for Claire. When they're waiting, Maria's mum phones her. Maria tells her mum about her day, but then they say goodbye and Maria wants to cry again.

'Maria, are you OK?' Emilia asks.

'Yes, perhaps, you know, Claire said it this morning?'

'Homesick?'

'Yes, homesick,' says Maria.

Emilia gives Maria a hug and says, 'It's OK, Maria. We're going to have the best time!'

'We're going to have the best time!'

Chapter 3

Jack

For the next four days, Maria and Emilia do everything together. Maria's English begins to get better because she and Emilia talk all the time. She talks more with students from their class, too. Sometimes, when they're talking, they don't know the words, but no one laughs. They all help. And so she isn't afraid now.

Every day, Maria and Emilia learn more about English people. The English say sorry all the time, and they put milk in their tea! Nothing closes in the afternoon like in Spain – and the people in shops call you 'love'. Maria likes that. She begins to like all the new things.

Claire doesn't cook potatoes once. She makes Thai food and Italian food, and Maria and Emilia help her. When Maria's mum calls on Thursday, Maria tells her all about her week, and she doesn't feel homesick when she says goodbye.

On Friday evening, the girls arrive back at Claire's house from school and there's a boy in the kitchen.

'Hi, girls!' Claire says. 'This is my sister's son, Jack. Would you like to go to Camden Market with him this weekend? You can buy some really good things there.'

Maria looks at Jack. He's about sixteen and tall, with blue eyes and a big smile. Very English and very handsome.

'Hi, Emilia. Hi, Maria,' says Jack.

'Hi, Jack,' says Emilia.

'Hi,' says Maria.

'Are you having a good time in London?' Jack asks. He's looking at Maria, but Emilia answers.

'Yes. We love it,' she says.

Jack is very English and very handsome.

'That's cool. How long are you here? Three weeks?'

'Now, two weeks and two days,' says Emilia.

Maria listens to them, but she doesn't speak. She doesn't want this boy to hear her bad English.

'So, do you want to go to Camden Market?' asks Jack.

'Yes, please!' says Emilia.

'Tomorrow morning?' says Jack.

'That's great,' Emilia says.

'Cool,' says Jack. 'Well, I need to go now. Can you be ready at ten o'clock?'

'Yes, of course,' says Emilia, and Jack leaves.

That night, Maria can't sleep because she's thinking about Jack. She feels sick and excited. What is she going to say to him? And what is she going to wear? She bought a new T-shirt with Emilia on Tuesday – perhaps she can wear that. Or her MLS T-shirt? MLS are her favourite band, but do people in England know them?

* * *

In the morning, Jack arrives for the girls and they take the Tube to Camden. Camden Market is amazing, and there's lots of music and food. People are wearing the coolest things.

'Shall we get a coffee?' Jack asks.

'Good idea,' says Emilia.

They find a coffee shop and get three coffees.

'So, where are you from in Spain and Poland?' asks Jack, when they sit down.

Camden Market is amazing, and there's lots of music and food.

'I'm from Warsaw and Maria is from Pamplona,' says Emilia. 'And are you… were you born in London?'

'I was,' says Jack. 'And I love it here.'

Emilia and Jack talk about London. Jack tells Emilia about his favourite things and places. Maria can understand Jack, and that feels good, but she doesn't speak to him. She's afraid, because she doesn't want to say the wrong thing.

'I want to go shopping!' says Emilia. She looks across the street. 'I'm going to look in that shop. You finish your coffees.' And she leaves Jack and Maria alone.

They both say nothing for a minute. Then Maria thinks of a question for Jack and she begins to ask it, but he begins talking, too. They laugh.

'You first,' says Jack.

'No, you!' says Maria.

'Well, you're wearing an MLS T-shirt,' Jack says. 'They're my favourite band. Do you like them?'

'You know MLS?' asks Maria.

'Of course! They're the best.'

'I love them too,' Maria says. 'What's your favourite song?'

'I love the song *Leaving Last*.'

'*Leaving Last*?' Maria says. 'No! *Fast Train* is the best song.'

Jack laughs. 'They're in London next week, you know.'

'MLS?' says Maria.

'Yes. They're doing a gig in London.'

Maria doesn't understand. 'A gig?' she says.

'Sorry,' says Jack. 'They're playing their music here in London. People are going to go and watch them.'

'Here?' says Maria, excited. 'Are you going to go?'

'No. I wanted to get tickets, but people bought them really fast. Everyone wants to go.'

'I'd really like to see MLS in a… gig? Is that right?' Maria says. 'But they never come to Pamplona.'

Maria looks up, and Emilia is standing next to the table.

'OK, shall we go shopping?' Jack says.

'Yes! Let's go!' says Maria.

They look in the shops and talk all day, but at four o'clock, Jack leaves the girls because he's meeting some friends. Before he goes, he asks, 'What are you doing tomorrow?'

'Nothing,' says Maria. She wants to see him again.

'Cool. Do you both want to do something?' he asks.

'Yes, please,' says Maria.

Jack takes Maria's phone number and says, 'OK, let's speak tomorrow.'

After he leaves, Emilia says, 'He likes you, Maria.'

'What? No!' says Maria. But Emilia smiles and says, 'He does. He likes you!'

Chapter 4
Brighton

The next morning, Maria and Emilia have breakfast alone, because Claire is out at the shops. Every five minutes, Maria looks at her phone. Emilia laughs.

'Maria! Stop looking at your phone!'

Maria puts her phone on the table, but after a minute, she looks again. Nothing. And then suddenly:

> Hi, Maria. It's Jack. What do you and Emilia want to do today? Perhaps we can go to Brighton? 😎

She gives her phone to Emilia. 'What do you think?' she asks.

'Maria! Stop looking at your phone!'

'Let's ask Claire,' says Emilia. They send a message to Claire, and she answers quickly:

> Great idea! Weather is going to be good. You can go to the beach. It's only an hour on the train.

Maria and Emilia meet Jack at the station in Clapham. He smiles his big smile when he sees them, and Maria's face goes red. She doesn't want to be quiet again, but when she looks at Jack, she forgets all her English.

It's better on the train. Jack teaches the girls some cool new words in English, like 'see you' for goodbye and 'cheers' for thank you. Soon Maria feels OK again.

When they arrive in Brighton, Jack takes the girls to The Lanes. It's a place with lots of little shops, and lots of cafés with tables on the street.

'There are lots of vintage shops here,' Jack says. 'Do you understand "vintage"? Old but really cool.'

That's strange, Maria thinks. You can't buy old things in the shops in Pamplona. The shops there have new things. Who wants to buy old things? But when she looks in one of the vintage shops, she's surprised. Some of the things are really nice, and she buys a book and a T-shirt.

They come out of The Lanes and walk past a very strange building. It looks Indian, not English.

'That's Brighton Pavilion,' Jack says, and he tells them about the building. He visited it with his school,

'That's Brighton Pavilion,' Jack says.

so he knows a lot about it. Maria wants to listen to him, but Emilia is between her and Jack, and there are lots of people, so she can't hear. Emilia was wrong, Maria thinks. Jack doesn't like me. He likes her.

From the Pavilion, they walk to the beach. There are lots of people there, and some are in the sea.

'In summer, everybody comes from London to Brighton,' Jack says.

There's a long building in front of them. It goes from the beach into the sea.

'That's Brighton Pier,' says Jack. 'Come on. Let's go there now.'

On the pier, there are some rollercoasters. Emilia, Jack, and Maria all want to go on the biggest rollercoaster, called *Turbo*. They buy tickets, but when Maria is getting her ticket, Jack and Emilia stand and talk quietly together. Then, when they get on the rollercoaster, Emilia sits next to Jack, and Maria sits alone. She can hear Jack and Emilia, and they are talking and laughing together. Why is Emilia doing this? Maria thinks. She feels hot and angry.

After the rollercoaster, they go back to the beach. Maria doesn't want to feel sad, so she smiles and laughs with Jack and Emilia, and she and Emilia teach Jack some Spanish and Polish. Jack is learning to say *Cómo estás?* ('How are you?' in Spanish), when Emilia suddenly looks at her phone.

Emilia sits next to Jack, and Maria sits alone.

'My boyfriend is calling me,' she says. 'Wait here, please?'

Emilia answers her phone and then walks up the beach, and Maria is alone with Jack. He asks her about Spain, and about her school and her friends and family. He wants to know everything about her. When she finishes talking, he looks at her carefully and says, 'You have beautiful eyes.'

For a second or two, Maria can't speak. Then she says, 'Cheers,' and Jack laughs.

'*You have beautiful eyes.*'

Emilia comes back, and they walk to the station. Maria stops for a second or two because she wants to look in a shop window, and at once Jack and Emilia talk quietly together again. So when Jack goes into a shop for some water, Maria says to Emilia, 'Why did you leave me alone on the rollercoaster?'

'I'm sorry,' says Emilia. 'Jack wanted to talk to me.'

'Why?' asks Maria.

'I can't tell you. I'm sorry,' says Emilia, but she's smiling, and she looks pleased about something.

Maria wants to ask Emilia more, but Jack comes out of the shop, and then they need to run to the station for their train.

They say goodbye to Jack at Claire's house, and go in and tell her about their day. All evening, when Maria looks at Emilia, Emilia is smiling at her.

'What is it, Emilia?' Maria asks. 'Why are you smiling like that?'

But every time, Emilia says, 'It's nothing!' and then talks about something different.

* * *

The next day, Monday, Maria looks at her phone after every class. She wants Jack to send her a message.

'Send a message to him!' says Emilia, but Maria is afraid. She looks at her phone again. Nothing.

At half past three that afternoon, Jack sends her a message! His mum and dad are out that night, he says, so he needs to stay in with his younger brother. But he wants to go to a café in Piccadilly Circus with Maria and Emilia on Tuesday evening.

All that night, and all the next day, Maria can't stop thinking about Jack. She can't forget her time alone on the beach with him. But then she thinks about him and Emilia on the rollercoaster. He's always nice to Maria and he asks her a lot of questions, but he asks Emilia questions, too. How does he feel about her? She needs to know!

Chapter 5
MLS

On Tuesday evening, Maria and Emilia are walking to the café when Emilia gets a message.

'It's my boyfriend,' says Emilia. 'He wants to talk. I need to go back to Claire's house and call him. Sorry.'

'Do you want to call him here?' says Maria. 'I can wait for you.'

'Thanks, Maria, but it's easier there. You go. You and Jack alone. That's good. I can send Jack a message.'

When Maria arrives at the café, Jack isn't there. Suddenly, Maria feels very nervous. Is Jack going to want to be alone with her? She waits for him, and looks at her phone every minute. She feels sick. Perhaps he isn't going to come, she thinks. But then he walks in with that big smile, and sits down.

'Sorry I'm late! How are you? How was your day?' he says.

They talk about school and music. It's good, but Jack usually talks a lot, and today he's much quieter. He doesn't want to be here, Maria thinks.

Suddenly Jack says, 'Maria, I want to tell you—'

But before he can finish, two students from Maria's class walk into the café.

'Maria! Hi! How are you?' they say.

'Jack, this is Sachi and Diego,' Maria says.

Sachi and Diego sit down at Maria and Jack's table.

Everybody says hello, and Sachi and Diego sit down at Maria and Jack's table. All the students in Maria's class like talking to English people, and they have lots of questions for Jack.

Jack smiles and talks to them, but after an hour, he says, 'I need to go now, Maria. My mum and dad are taking me out for dinner tonight.'

Maria goes with Jack to the door of the café.

'Can you get back to Claire's house OK?' Jack asks.

'Yes, of course,' Maria says. 'What did you want to say, Jack?'

'What?'

'Before?' she says.

He smiles nervously. 'Nothing. It doesn't matter. See you soon, Maria.'

When Maria arrives back at Claire's house, Emilia looks excited, and she asks, 'How was your evening? Did you talk to Jack?'

'Yes, but Sachi and Diego came and sat with us. So we didn't talk a lot,' says Maria. 'Is everything OK with Aurek?'

'I don't know,' Emilia says, and now her face is sad. 'It isn't easy, me here and Aurek in Poland.'

Emilia goes to bed early, and Maria feels sad for her. But she can't stop thinking about Jack again. What did

'It isn't easy, me here and Aurek in Poland.'

he want to tell her? Perhaps he was quiet because he wanted to see Emilia. Or perhaps he didn't like Sachi and Diego. Maria needs to know! And she isn't going to see him for three days now, because he's out with his friends and family for the next two nights, and on Friday she's going out with Emilia.

The next two days go slowly. Emilia and Maria go out with their new friends from summer school in the evenings. Emilia is quiet, and she's on the phone to Aurek a lot. On Friday, Emilia needs to stay and finish some work after school, so Maria goes back to Claire's house alone. She's watching TV when Claire opens the door and says, 'Maria, Jack is here. He wants to see you.'

Maria goes into the kitchen, and Jack is standing there. He looks very excited and he has two tickets.

'Maria! Look!' he says. 'I've got tickets for MLS. A friend gave them to me.' She looks at the tickets.

'For tonight? That's great, Jack!'

'I know!' he says.

'Please take a video for me, Jack,' says Maria.

'What? A video? Maria, you're coming with me!'

'With you?' she says.

'Yes. I have two tickets! My friend and his girlfriend can't go. You love MLS. Let's go together.'

'Oh, Jack!' says Maria, excited. Then she remembers something. 'Wait. I can't. Emilia and I are going out tonight.'

'Tell her about the tickets,' Jack says.

Maria calls Emilia, but there's no answer. She calls again. No answer. What can she do? She wants to see the band. MLS are never going to come to Pamplona – and she wants to go with Jack. She calls a third time. No answer.

'What time is the gig?' she asks.

'It begins at seven o'clock, so we need to leave soon.'

Maria tells Claire about the MLS gig, and then she sends a message to Emilia.

> Emi, Jack got MLS tickets for tonight! 😊 I really want to go with him. Can we do something tomorrow? Really sorry.

* * *

MLS are amazing. They play Maria's favourite song, and Jack's, and Jack and Maria have the best time together. But Maria feels bad when she thinks about Emilia alone at Claire's house. She looks at her phone, but there is no answer from Emilia. After the last song, Jack takes Maria's hand.

'Maria. I want to tell you something.'

'Is everything OK?' she asks.

'Everything is amazing. I want to say…'

Jack is quiet, and Maria looks at him. 'What?'

'I want to tell you…'

'Jack? What is it?'

Jack and Maria have the best time together.

'Maria, I like you,' he says. 'I like you a lot.'

Maria can't breathe. Then Jack kisses her. And she feels like the happiest person in London.

Jack and Maria get the Tube after the gig and then they walk to Claire's house, hand in hand. When they get to Claire's, Maria says, 'I had the best night. Thank you, Jack!' Then she laughs because she feels nervous again.

'Can I see you tomorrow?' he asks.

'Yes. I want to see you.'

'OK,' he says. 'In the morning?'

'The morning is good. See you.'

And then he kisses her again.

'Goodnight, Maria.'

Maria runs into the house. She wants to tell Emilia everything. But it's late, and there's nobody downstairs.

Maria goes upstairs, but Claire and Emilia's doors are closed. So she goes into her room, and gets ready for bed. She doesn't sleep for hours, because she can't stop thinking about Jack, and she has MLS songs in her head.

Chapter 6
London Bus

When Maria goes downstairs for breakfast on Saturday morning, Emilia is there.

'Emilia! Last night was amazing!' Maria says.

Emilia doesn't answer or look up.

'Jack and I... it was amazing!' she says again.

'I heard.'

Maria doesn't understand.

'What's the matter, Emilia?' she says. 'I called you, but you didn't answer. So then I sent you a message. I wanted to tell you about Jack and me last night, but you were in bed.'

Emilia looks up, and her eyes are red. 'Aurek finished with me last night. He is not my boyfriend now.'

'What? Why?' says Maria. 'Oh, Emilia, I'm sorry. Are you OK?'

'I needed you.'

'I didn't know. I'm sorry,' Maria says.

'I sent you a message,' says Emilia.

'I didn't get it. I'm sorry. Why did he...?'

Now Emilia is crying.

'Oh, Emilia!' Maria hugs Emilia. Then she hears somebody at the door. Jack!

'Can you answer the door, girls?' Claire calls. Maria doesn't want to leave Emilia, but then someone calls

Emilia's phone, and she answers, so Maria goes to the door. Jack is there and he's smiling, but Emilia is crying and Maria can't leave her.

'Jack, I can't see you today,' Maria says. 'I'm sorry.' She tells him about Emilia.

'But you leave in a week!' he says.

'I know, but Emilia needs me. Can I call you later?'

'OK,' he says, and he leaves, but he doesn't kiss her. For a minute, Maria wants to run down the street after him. But she thinks of Emilia, and she goes back into the house.

Emilia is crying and talking to her mum on her phone. Maria finds Claire.

'I feel really bad for Emilia, Claire. What can I do?'

'Jack, I can't see you today,' Maria says.

'She's OK, Maria,' says Claire. 'She's going to come with me in a minute. We're going to do some shopping for an hour or two.'

That gives Maria an idea. 'Claire,' she says, 'can I cook something? And we can eat together when you get back?'

'That's a nice idea, Maria,' says Claire.

'OK, see you back here later,' says Maria. And she gets out her phone, looks for something, and then finds her bag and leaves the house.

* * *

She's nearly ready when Claire and Emilia arrive back at the house.

'What's that smell?' asks Emilia when she walks into the house. 'It's like home.'

'It's *borscht*,' Maria tells her.

'What?'

'It's *borscht*. I made it for you,' she says.

'You made *borscht*?' says Emilia. 'For me?'

'Yes,' says Maria. 'But it wasn't easy, because I didn't know the English word for that big red vegetable. Bee…, beet…'

'Beetroot!' Claire laughs. 'So it's a beetroot soup? It looks amazing, Maria. Let's eat it!'

Emilia hugs Maria, and they sit down with Claire and eat together. After the *borscht*, Maria and Emilia go to Emilia's room.

'You made borscht? For me?'

'What happened with Aurek?' Maria asks.

'I don't want to think about him. Tell me about Jack.'

Maria tells Emilia about the gig and the kiss.

'I knew it!' says Emilia. 'You know, when we were on the rollercoaster in Brighton, he asked me, "Does Maria have a boyfriend?" He asked me all about you. But he said "Don't tell Maria," so I couldn't tell you. Do you like him, Maria?'

'Of course! He's amazing.'

'Where is he now?' asks Emilia.

'I don't know.'

'What? Call him,' says Emilia. 'He needs to come and have some *borscht*.'

'No. I want to be with you today,' says Maria.

'Really?' asks Emilia.

'Yes. What do you want to do?'

'I've got an idea!' says Emilia. 'Remember on the first day, we both wanted to go on a red bus? Let's do it this afternoon.'

'Yes! Let's!' says Maria.

* * *

They go on a big red bus. They see Buckingham Palace and Trafalgar Square, then they go over the River Thames and see Tower Bridge and the Tower of London, Big Ben, and the London Eye.

'I love this city,' Maria says.

'Me too.'

'Let's come back one day, you and me?'

'Yes,' says Emilia. 'Yes, let's.'

When the girls get back to Claire's house, Jack is there.

'Jack, what are you doing here?' asks Maria.

'Emilia sent me a message,' says Jack.

'Did you?' Maria asks Emilia.

'Yes,' she says. 'This is our last week. I want to see you, but Jack wants to see you, too.'

Maria hugs Emilia and says in her ear, 'You're the best, Emilia. Thank you.'

'I love this city.'

Chapter 7
Goodbye England

Maria's last week in London is wonderful. She has her classes with Emilia, and after class, she sees Jack, or she does something with Emilia and Jack. And then suddenly, it's the last day. Claire drives Maria and Emilia to the airport, and Jack goes too.

First, Maria says goodbye to Claire. 'Thank you for everything, Claire. You're my English mum.'

'And you're my Spanish daughter!' says Claire. 'Have a good flight, and come and see us again soon.' She hugs Maria.

Second is Jack. Now Maria is crying. 'Jack,' she says, 'I'm going to miss you.'

'I'm going to miss you too,' he says.

'But you're going to come to Spain?'

'Yes. And you must come back here soon too,' he says.

'Of course,' says Maria. 'See you, Jack.'

'Goodbye, Maria.' And he kisses her.

Last is Emilia. Both girls are crying.

'Come to Poland soon!' says Emilia. 'You can eat my mum's *borscht*.' Maria laughs, and the girls hug.

'See you, Maria. You're an amazing friend.'

'You too, Emilia,' says Maria.

They hug one last time and then Maria has to go.

Maria and Emilia hug.

When Maria gets on the plane and sits down, she thinks about her mum and dad, her friends, her brother, and her dog, and Spanish food, and she begins to feel excited. A woman is sitting next to her, and she has an English book about Pamplona.

'Do you know Pamplona?' Maria asks.

The woman smiles. 'No, I don't. This is my first visit. And you?'

'It's my city,' says Maria. 'I live there.'

'Really?' says the woman. 'Can you tell me about it?'

So Maria tells the woman about her favourite things and places in Pamplona. She tells her about *tortilla de bacalao*, her favourite food. And in her head, she thinks, Goodbye England!

Goodbye England!

alone *(adj & adv)* without any people

amazing *(adj)* exciting and interesting

band *(n)* a music group

beach *(n)* a place next to the sea, with sand or little stones

both *(det)* the two; not only one but also the other

breathe *(v)* to take air in and out through your nose and mouth

bus *(n)* a big vehicle; it takes a lot of people along the road and stops often, and then people get on and off

buy *(v)* to give money because you want something

carpet *(n)* in a room, a soft covering over all the floor

chips *(n)* thin pieces of potato; you cook them in oil

city *(n)* a big and important town

cook *(v)* to make hot food; **cooking** *(n)*

cool *(adj)* great, amazing, and different

egg *(n)* food from a chicken; it is hard and round, and soft inside

escalator *(n)* moving stairs; they take people up and down in a building

favourite *(adj)* one thing that you like best of all

fish *(n)* an animal that you can eat; it lives in water

flat *(n)* a home in a house or big building; there are usually more flats above, below, or next door

flight *(n)* when you go somewhere in a plane

great *(adj)* very, very good

hug *(v & n)* to put your arms around somebody

idea *(n)* a plan or new thought; something new in your head

kiss *(v & n)* to touch somebody with your lips (part of your mouth) when you want to show love

kitchen *(n)* a room in a house; you cook food there

message *(n)* words from one person to another

miss *(v)* to feel sad about somebody or something because they are not there

music *(n)* when you sing or play an instrument, e.g. the guitar

nervous *(adj)* worried or afraid

place *(n)* where something or somebody is, e.g. in a building, town, or country

potato *(n)* a white vegetable; it grows underground

rollercoaster *(n)* a small train at a fair or fun park; it goes up and down and around for fun

sad *(adj)* not happy

sausage *(n)* a kind of meat

send *(v)* When you send something, e.g. a letter or a message, it goes from one place/person to another.

show *(n)* You watch a show at the theatre or on television.

sick *(adj)* not well

smell *(v & n)* to notice something (know it is there) with your nose

song *(n)* music with words

soup *(n)* vegetables or meat cooked in water, that you can eat or drink

station *(n)* where trains stop and people get on and off

strange *(adj)* surprising; not usual

surprised *(adj)* how people feel when something happens suddenly

tea *(n)* a hot drink; it comes from the leaves of a plant

together *(adv)* with someone or with people

Tube *(n)* the underground trains in London

underground *(adj & adv)* under the top part of the earth

vegetable *(n)* food (e.g. a potato or a bean) that grows in the ground

word *(n)* what we say when we speak and write

BEYOND THE STORY

Visit London by Bus

Take a red bus around London. The bus goes to all the famous places in the city, and you can get on and off when you want. You can visit…

Big Ben & The Houses of Parliament ▶

The Houses of Parliament are the home of the UK government. The Parliament Clock Tower has the world's biggest clock with four 'faces'. People often call the tower 'Big Ben', but 'Big Ben' is not the name of the tower. It is the name of the bell in the tower.

◀ The Tower of London

The Tower of London is almost 1,000 years old, and it is a very interesting and exciting place. It is famous for its ravens. These big black birds live in the tower. Visitors can see the Crown Jewels here, too.

Trafalgar Square ▶

Trafalgar Square is a very famous place in London. People often meet here, and look at the many pigeons, grey and white birds.

◀ Tower Bridge

Tower Bridge goes over the River Thames near The Tower of London. It can go up when big ships need to go down the river.

....

Buckingham Palace ▶

Buckingham Palace is home to the Queen. People can visit the palace and see its beautiful gardens.

....

◀ The London Eye

The London Eye is next to the River Thames. It is 135 metres tall. It takes 30 minutes to go around and you can see across London.

....

READ & DISCUSS Read the guide for Maria and Emilia's bus tour. Answer the questions.

1 Where would you like to visit on the bus? Why?

2 Where would you not like to visit? Why?

bridge *(n)* a way across a road or river for cars, people, and trains

crown jewels *(n)* headwear and beautiful stones for a king/queen

government *(n)* A country's government decides all the important things for the country.

queen *(n)* the most important woman in a country

river *(n)* a long narrow waterway to/from the sea

tower *(n)* a tall narrow building or a tall part of a building

Think Ahead

1 Look at the story title, cover, and contents page. Correct the <u>underlined</u> words in the sentences.

   1 The story happens in <u>spring</u>.
   2 Maria wants to learn <u>Polish</u>.
   3 The boy in the story is called <u>James</u>.
   4 Maria stays in <u>Pamplona</u>.
   5 Maria's best friend in London is called <u>Claire</u>.

2 What is going to happen in the story? Can you guess?

   1 Maria gets a boyfriend.
   2 Maria likes Jack, and Emilia likes Jack, too.
   3 Maria doesn't want to go back to Spain.

3 **RESEARCH** Before you read, find the answers to these questions.

   1 This story happens in London and Brighton. How can you get to Brighton from London? How long does it take?
   2 What can a visitor see and do in Brighton?

Chapter Check

CHAPTER 1 Choose the correct words to complete the sentences.

1 Maria leaves Pamplona in the *morning* / *evening*.

2 She is going to stay in England for *two* / *three* weeks.

3 Emilia looks *excited* / *nervous* when she meets Maria.

4 Claire asks the girls about their favourite *music* / *food*.

5 The houses in Claire's street are all *white* / *brown*.

6 School begins at *eight fifteen* / *nine o'clock*.

CHAPTER 2 Are the sentences true or false?

1 Maria is sleeping when she hears Emilia crying.

2 Maria likes cooking, and Emilia likes cooking, too.

3 The students in the girls' class are all Polish.

4 Maria likes her fish and chips.

5 Emilia has an English boyfriend.

6 Emilia is nice to Maria when she misses her family.

CHAPTER 3 Put the events in order.

a Jack takes Maria's phone number.

b Jack and Maria talk about their favourite music.

c Jack takes Maria and Emilia to a coffee shop.

d Emilia says, 'He likes you.'

e Emilia goes shopping without Jack or Maria.

CHAPTER 3 Correct the underlined words.

1 Jack looks very <u>Spanish</u>.

2 Jack wants to meet the girls at <u>eleven</u> o'clock.

3 They go to Camden on the <u>bus</u>.

4 <u>Maria's</u> favourite MLS song is *Leaving Last*.

CHAPTER 4 Complete the sentences with the place names below. There is one extra place.

Brighton Pavilion   Brighton Pier   Clapham
Piccadilly Circus   The Lanes

1 In Brighton, there are vintage shops and cafés in
   _____.

2 _____ looks like an Indian building.

3 Jack, Maria, and Emilia go on a rollercoaster on
   _____.

4 Jack wants to meet the girls in a café in _____
   on Tuesday.

CHAPTER 4 Who says these things? Write the correct name next to each one.

Claire Emilia Jack Maria

1 'Stop looking at your phone!' _____

2 'You can go to the beach.' _____

3 'You have beautiful eyes.' _____

4 'Why are you smiling like that?' _____

CHAPTER 5 Match the sentence halves.

1 Emilia goes back to Claire's house…

2 Jack wants to tell Maria something, …

3 In the evenings, the girls go out…

4 Jack wants Maria to go…

5 Maria calls Emilia, …

a with friends from summer school.

b but she does not answer.

c to the MLS gig with him.

d because her boyfriend calls.

e but Sachi and Diego start talking to them.

CHAPTER 6 Complete the sentences with the names of people in the story. You will need to use some of the names more than once.

Aurek   Claire   Emilia   Jack   Maria

1 _____ is sad because _____ is not her boyfriend now.

2 _____ sent a message, but _____ didn't get it.

3 _____ tells _____, 'I can't see you today.'

4 _____ goes shopping and _____ goes with her.

5 _____ makes *borscht* for _____ and _____.

CHAPTER 6 Choose the correct words to complete the sentences.

1 Jack *kisses / doesn't kiss* Maria when he leaves.

2 *Borscht* is Emilia's favourite *Spanish / Polish* food.

3 Emilia doesn't want to talk about *Jack / Aurek*.

4 The girls go around London on *the Tube / a bus*.

5 When the girls get home, Jack is there because *Maria / Emilia* sent him a message.

CHAPTER 7 Correct the underlined words.

1 Claire takes Maria and Emilia to the <u>station</u>.

2 Jack is going to <u>leave</u> Maria.

3 Emilia wants Maria to come to <u>England</u> soon.

4 The woman on the plane has an English book about <u>London</u>.

CHAPTER 7 Tick (✓) the three true sentences.

1 Claire wants Maria to visit her again.

2 Jack doesn't say goodbye to Maria.

3 Jack is going to go to Poland.

4 Maria cries when she leaves her friends.

5 Maria feels excited because she's going home.

Focus on Vocabulary

1 Match the words below with their meanings.

sausage a big and important town

band music with words

city a kind of meat

song a music group

2 Replace the <u>underlined</u> words with the words below.

alone   beetroot   hugs   sad   strange

1 At first, England feels <u>unusual and different</u> to Maria.

2 Maria feels sad because she is <u>not with other people</u>.

3 Emilia is <u>not happy</u> because she misses Aurek.

4 *Borscht* is a soup with <u>a red vegetable</u> in it.

5 Claire <u>puts her arms around</u> Maria at the airport.

3 Complete the text with the correct words.

amazing   gig   kiss   misses   nervous   together

When Maria arrives in England, she feels ¹_____ and she ²_____ her family. But a girl called Emilia is staying at the house in England with her. They go to a summer school and they have a lot of fun ³_____. Then Maria meets Jack. He takes the girls to Brighton and he takes Maria to an MLS ⁴_____. They have an ⁵_____ time, and at the end of the evening, they ⁶_____.

Focus on Language

1 **Complete each sentence with the present simple or present continuous form of a verb below.**

cry   get   ~~think~~   wait   walk   want

Maria can't sleep because she _is thinking_ about Jack.

1 When Maria arrives in London, Claire _____ for her.

2 Maria gets out of bed because someone _____.

3 Sometimes Maria _____ things wrong when she speaks English.

4 Emilia gets a message when they _____ to the café.

5 Jack _____ Maria to go to the MLS gig with him.

2 **Complete the sentences with the -*ing* or infinitive form of the verb in brackets.**

Maria can't stop _thinking_ (think) about her mum and dad.

1 Now she needs _____ (get) on the plane.

2 It's beginning _____ (get) dark.

3 'Maria! Stop _____ (look) at your phone!'

4 She doesn't want _____ (speak) English.

5 When Maria finishes _____ (talk), Jack says, 'You have beautiful eyes.'

3 **DECODE** Read this text from the story. Look at the underlined pronouns 1–5. Which person/people do they describe? Choose the correct answers.

When Maria arrives back at Claire's house, Emilia looks excited, and ⁽¹⁾ she asks, 'How was your evening? Did you talk to Jack?'

'Yes, but Sachi and Diego came and sat with us. So ⁽²⁾ we didn't talk a lot,' says Maria. 'Is everything OK with Aurek?'

'I don't know,' Emilia says, and now ⁽³⁾ her face is sad. 'It isn't easy, me here and Aurek in Poland.'

Emilia goes to bed early, and Maria feels sad for ⁽⁴⁾ her. But she can't stop thinking about Jack again. What did ⁽⁵⁾ he want to tell her?

1 a Claire   b Emilia   c Maria

2 a Emilia and Maria
   b Maria and Jack
   c Sachi and Diego

3 a Maria's   b Claire's   c Emilia's

4 a Emilia   b Maria   c Claire

5 a Aurek   b Jack   c Diego

Discussion

1 (COLLABORATE) Work with a partner. Look at the adjectives from the story. Do they describe positive (good) or negative (bad) feelings? Mark them + (positive) or – (negative).

angry   excited   homesick   nervous   sad   surprised

2 (COMMUNICATE) What do the adjectives in exercise 1 mean? Discuss with your partner.

3 Read the situations from the story. Match an adjective from exercise 1 with each situation to show how Maria is feeling.

Maria feels that everything is strange and different in England, and she wants to be in Spain. *homesick*

1 At breakfast, there is bread and coffee like in Spain – not sausages and eggs.

2 Maria needs to speak English every day in London, and she can't speak Spanish.

3 Emilia sits next to Jack on the rollercoaster – but she has a boyfriend in Poland.

4 Jack gives Maria a ticket for the MLS concert.

5 Maria says goodbye to Claire, Emilia, and Jack.

4 Match the reasons below with the adjectives and situations in exercise 3.

Maria feels like this because…

a MLS are her favourite band.

b her friend Isabella had sausages and eggs for breakfast every day in England.

c she is going to miss them.

d Maria really likes Jack, and Emilia knows that.

e she doesn't want to say the wrong thing.

5 **COMMUNICATE** Choose one positive and one negative feeling from exercise 1. When did you last feel like this? Tell your partner. Say why.

6 **COMMUNICATE** Work with your partner. Imagine you are going to a summer school in England for three weeks. Read the sentences below. What do you think you are going to feel when these things happen? Why?

1 You arrive in England.

2 You have your first day at summer school.

3 You eat English food for the first time.

4 You speak English to other boys or girls.

1 Read the profile about a summer school. Would you like to go to this school? Why/Why not?

BAYVIEW SUMMER SCHOOL
Location: Brighton, England
Number of students: 160
Facilities: Student room with coffee/tea; computer room; café; shop
What to do in Brighton: visit the famous Brighton Pier; go to the beach; ride on the rollercoaster; enjoy shopping and cafés in The Lanes; go to London for the day

2 You are going to a summer school in England. Where would you like to go? Research these cities and choose your favourite.

Oxford

Manchester

Bristol

Liverpool

3 What facilities would you like at your summer school? What would you like to do there? Write a profile for your school. Use the profile in exercise 1 as a guide.

4 THINK CRITICALLY Work in groups. Take turns to describe your summer schools. Decide as a group which school is the best. Why?

5 COLLABORATE In your groups, prepare a short presentation for the class on the school you decided was the best.

6 Have a class vote to decide which summer school is the most popular.

If you liked this Bookworm, why not try...

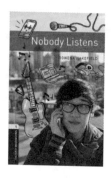

Nobody Listens

STAGE 1
Rowena Wakefield

Alex's family are always moving from town to town. He doesn't make new friends now, because he doesn't like saying goodbye to them. He has his music, his songs, and his guitar, and they're only for him. It's best like that, he thinks.

Then he meets Bella, and everything gets difficult. He likes her. He likes her very much. But she wants him to play his music for everyone. And how can he say goodbye to her, when his parents decide to move again?

The Summer Intern

STAGE 2
Helen Salter

Anna wants to be a writer, so when she gets a summer job at a fashion and beauty website called *Gloss*, she's very excited. But things are not easy. Anna's best friend Katie is upset with her, her mother phones her every day at work, and Tina, the editor of *Gloss*, wants her to make the coffee and pick up the post, not write features. 'Am I ever going to write something for *Gloss*?' Anna thinks. 'And how am I going to get my best friend back, and explain to my mum that I'm fifteen, not five?'